SIMPLY REDEEMED

From Prison to Purpose

ANGELA BROWN

@2025 by Angela Brown
Uncaused Publishing
Orlando, FL

Printed in the United States of America

All rights reserved. No part of this publication may be reproduced, stored in a retrieval system, or transmitted in any form or by any means – for example, electronic, photocopy, recording – without the prior written permission of the publisher. The only exception is brief quotations in printed reviews.

Brown, Angela

Simply Redeemed

ISBN: 979-8-9898982-9-9

CONTENTS

Foreword 5

Acknowledgements 7

1. How Did I Get Here? 9

2. The Woman with the Issue of Drugs 17

3. From Perversion to Power 29

4. The Graveyard 43

5. From Guilt to Grace 49

6. The Miracle of Ministry 57

About the Author 71

FOREWORD

My sincere prayer and desire is that this book finds you in good health, wealth, and spiritual prosperity. If by some chance you're not there yet I am positive you will be headed in the right direction after reading this book.

Angela Brown has acquired all these qualities attributes and abilities due to her bold faith, courage, and desire to see the people of God and herself thrive in a world that is wicked, weird, and wounded.

I have had the honor of being this woman of God's Pastor and Bishop for 8 years on the blessed side of her story and I can tell you that her transparency, unapologetic honesty, and integrity that were birthed from her traumatic experiences through her desire to please God, and ultimately the action of turning her life over despite what she came through.

May God grant the same favor on you as you read this book and your own testimony be read, heard and felt in due season.

Peace and blessings,
Bishop D.L. Williams
Founder of Apostolics of Byron Church in Byron Ga

ACKNOWLEDGEMENTS

I would like to thank first and foremost my Lord and Savior Jesus Christ who knows my beginning and end. I want to give a special thank you to Bishop Williams who saw potential in me before I recognized it within myself. I give honor to my church The Apostolic Church of Byron which is located in Byron, GA. I give honor to all of my closest friends and family who have prayed with me and for me on this journey.

I love you all.
Angela Brown

HOW DID I GET HERE?

He longed to fill his stomach with the pods that the pigs were eating, but no one gave him anything.

LUKE 15:16 NIV

I had all the talent and ability to be a great success. God put so much potential within me, but how did I get here? I was drunk again. Numbing my pain with more cocaine. Neglecting my nephew to get another high. How did I get this low? I was born and raised in St. Petersburg, FL. My mom and dad had four children, two boys and two girls, and I was the second oldest. We grew up in a small 2-bedroom home, and we had two bunk beds, one for the girls and one for the boys. I had an active childhood and played many sports. I remember when my mom washed and hot-pressed my hair to get it all pretty. And later in the evening, my neighborhood guy friends would play football on the field. Then I would run over and get into the game and play with them, and my mom would be so mad because I messed up my hair. I was such a happy-go-lucky person. To this day, that is why I love football.

As a child, I saw my father abusing my mother. Every time my dad would drink it was normal to hear verbal abuse and even some physical abuse. It wasn't until I was much older that I realized that this type of behavior was not normal. For me it was a every other weekend when my dad got drunk. Have you ever been born into dysfunction? Where dysfunction is normal? I was raised in this dysfunction. As I grew older, I was not afraid of abuse or dysfunction. I was more afraid of healthy relationships and love. Have you ever witnessed so much pain that love, and kindness are weird to you? Disappointment and despair were my constant companions.

I thank God that my father turned his life around later in llfe. God did an incredible work in my father, he blessed all of his kids before he passed. The end of a thing is better than the beginning according to Scripture. He ended his race in the arms of Jesus and left a godly inheritance to his children. He allowed God to do a deep work upon his heart which impacts all of us to this day. Never stop praying for family. As long as they are breathing, there is still hope.

One day, when I was 13 years old, I visited a close friend's house. While there hanging out and playing around, I fell asleep. I woke up to this painful penetration of a stranger raping me. I yelled in utter disbelief. I was so confused about what was going on. I tried to fight him off, but it was too late. Whenever he was done with me, he walked out as if he did nothing wrong. I sat there in stunned silence. I did not know what to say or what to do. Internally, I blamed myself for falling asleep. I cried and pulled up my shorts and ran out of the home. I walked all the way home that day. I limped in pain as blood ran down my leg. I hurried home and took a bath. While in the shower I could still smell the stench and the sweat on my body. The pain of this moment followed me for years. Sometimes I would wince in pain whenever I thought of how he forced himself inside of me. He took my virginity. How did I get here? I was a virgin and had never been sexually active with anybody, and that was devastating to me. He took something that was innocent and precious to me. I was tormented in my mind and I was so afraid of telling anybody because he was a close family friend. I thought no one would believe me.

Young ladies, speak up if someone assaults you. You have power in your voice. I wish I would have spoken up, but I was so afraid. Thank God, I am speaking up now and empowering ladies to take their voice back. This man tried to rape me again every time we were in the same vicinity. I lived in utter fear of this guy. The fear of this man turned into a fear of all men. I began to withdraw from all men. These early traumatic moments birthed a deep hatred within me. I was afraid that every man I met was out to do some type of harm to me. I was being molded early by this trauma. A seed of perversion had been planted after that rape.

My household and this rape really shaped my thinking. The impact of the dysfunction and the rape would be seen for much of my life. I joined the Army to help my mom move away from the toxic environment created by my dad whenever he started drinking. I joined the army to improve my life and to help my mom. But while still serving in the Army, I got called into the office by my first sergeant. He hesitantly told me that Red Cross had called to inform him that my mother had died. My mother was only 52 years old when she passed. My precious mother had a heart attack and died. I was only 24 years old. How did I get here? I loved my mother and the loss of her sent me into a dark place. With her gone, I had to accept some responsibilities that I was not ready for. Before she passed, my mother had full custody of my nephew. My nephew was only two years old. I was the only one that was able to take him in. I was trying to figure out my own life, now I had to consider someone else's.

I started working two jobs in order to survive. I was working and partying. I started missing days of work due to partying and began neglecting my little nephew. I was snorting cocaine, smoking weed, and drinking all at the same time. I was drinking beer and any type of hard liquor I could find after I got out of the military. On weekends, I would visit clubs and attend parties. I was juggling two jobs while caring for my nephew. I was spiraling out of control. More responsibilities, more beer. More bills, more beer. The excess responsibilities that were on my shoulders left no time for me to grieve my mother's death. Unprepared and overwhelmed, I was expected to handle everything. My escape came through getting high and partying, which led to crack cocaine. I got addicted to crack cocaine in 1995, and it triggered a downfall into darkness despite having a supportive family.

Through all of the drugs and trauma that I endured, God never abandoned me. It makes me think of the story of the prodigal son. He departed the father's house and wasted his inheritance. He spent his money on prostitutes and terrible things. After spending all of his money he was in a pig's pen hungry. He was so hungry that he wanted what the pigs were eating. Finally, he came to himself and said that he would go back to his father's house and tell him that he was not worthy to be called his son. When the prodigal son started his journey back home, while he was still afar off the father came towards him running and embraced him. The father restored him as if nothing ever happened. What I realize about our Heavenly Father is that no matter how far we go away from him, when we start to seek him again. He truly meets us wherever we are. The prodigal son was still far away from his father, but his father made up the distance by running to him. Thank God for my Heavenly Father that would not stop pursuing me. How did I get here? Or the better question is, how did God meet me here?

> *So, he got up and went to his father. But while he was still a long way off, his father saw him and was filled with compassion for him; he ran to his son, threw his arms around him and kissed him.*
>
> LUKE 15:20 NIV

2

THE WOMAN WITH THE ISSUE OF DRUGS

"And a certain woman, which had an issue of blood twelve years, and had suffered many things of many physicians, and had spent all that she had, and was nothing bettered, but rather grew worse."

MARK 5:25-26 KJV

Whenever your life is down spiraling, you will try anything and everything. During this time of trial and pain, I really didn't read the Bible. But if there is a story in the Bible that I relate to, it is this one about the woman with the issue of blood. She had a condition which caused her to be pushed away from society and her family. No one knew how to heal her condition. She tried everything. She went to the best doctors and the best physicians, but she was not getting better. She was actually getting worse. Things got so bad that she finally took a step of faith and tried Jesus. My condition lasted longer than her condition, but my problem was not blood. My problem was drugs. I had developed an issue with drugs because nothing else was helping me while I was trying to survive the trauma of my mother passing away and me being raped. Perhaps it was my one anchor of safety that was jerked away from me, maybe that was the problem. I don't know, but what I do know is that I tried everything. I did not get better, I actually got even worse. As far as I can remember, I believe I started smoking weed and drinking at the early age of 13, all the while hiding it from my parents. My family bloodline drank alcohol and partied regularly. It looked harmless and cool to me because they worked and had jobs and homes. I was also a wild child, so I would try everything. Eventually, I started snorting cocaine, drinking, and smoking weed. My life began this aggressive decline. My attitude, my work ethic, and the care of my nephew. Everything suffered. All I wanted to do was get high. I lost my job, and I realized then I didn't want my family to know how strung out I was on crack cocaine. I started missing work and neglecting my nephew. I got into the habit of lying and stealing from family members and close friends. I could not handle the guilt and shame that I was living in. It was tearing at my soul. It seemed that all of my relationships fell apart. I loved my nephew, but I was too busy in my own chaos. One day, I woke up and left everyone and everything. I left my nephew with my dad. My auntie came to pick him up later. My aunt then took full custody of raising my nephew, thank God for that. I refused to tell anyone where I was going. I just wanted to disappear. I was too embarrassed to tell them that I had gotten addicted to crack cocaine.

I was so addicted to that drug that I stayed out there after being abused and raped several times. I had almost lost my mind. Most people think you are out there just having sex. That is far from the truth; it was more scheming and stealing from men. Especially if they came there to get high on crack. I remember just being asked to walk or dress a certain way for their entertainment, and once they started getting high, they were unable to perform or do anything, we would rob and take everything from them. I remember once robbing this rich guy, and afterwards he came looking for me and my friend because we always worked together. That is when I knew deep down inside, I had to get help, but I did not know how because I was playing some dangerous games.

A couple of weeks had passed since the incident of running from the rich man. I got into an argument with my girlfriend, Tina, because she was acting recklessly again. I went into the room and got the gun. I was ready to shoot her, but she ran which gave me time to calm down. I held the gun in my hand and I forgot that I had already cocked it back. She came back into the hotel room, and we made up. I held the gun in my hand while she pulled out more drugs. I laid the gun on the counter, and suddenly it went off. To this day, I do not know where that bullet went. It could have hit her, me, or someone else in the next room. But God was keeping me the entire time. Life out there was truly wild, it is easy to become just as wild.

Things got worse, I decided to leave with a man I barely knew. He sold vacuum cleaners' door-to-door. I started working with him since I didn't have a job anymore. My fresh start was with a vacuum cleaner. Perhaps this job could fill the vacuum within me that no drug could fill. Have you ever tried to fill the void with something you knew wouldn't help you in the long run? The more that you try to fill the void by yourself, it seems that you make matters worse. The more that you try to fix the problem yourself, the worse the problem seems to get. The woman with the issue of blood was not getting any better with her condition. The more she tried her own methods of healing, the worse that she got. This was a part of my life that the more I tried to fill the void, the worse my life got. I had an issue with drugs that I was too embarrassed to admit. I was in survival mode. Whenever you are in survival mode, you do some crazy things. Do y'all remember those vacuums called Kirby? I learned that there was also a vacuum cleaner called "Rainbow." I thought to myself, I can travel with this company and get myself together, little did I know this guy was doing crack cocaine as well. Everybody who was employed in this job was a drug addict, and we would get high every day after work. This was the very thing that I was trying to escape. The more I tried to fix my life, the worse things were getting. We were getting high together and I started doing things that I never dreamed that I would do. I started selling my body. I was desperate to buy more drugs. These drugs had a hold on my life. No matter how hard I tried to break free, I would go back to this bondage. I was prostituting my body to get more and more money to waste it on more drugs. Whenever I was in desperate need for more crack, I started robbing people. I would steal from friends and strangers. I truly had an issue that only God could fix.

The longer I lingered in this situation, the more my life began to down spiral. Have you ever stayed loyal to something that was destroying you inside and out? How about staying loyal to someone that was hurting you? The longer I remained in this relationship the more I acted out of character. I not only had an issue with drugs, but I had an issue with the possibility of abandonment. More than anything, I did not want to be alone. When you have abandonment issues, you will stay in a relationship even if it is toxic. The toxicity is more comfortable than the thought of being alone. This fear of abandonment caused me to abandon myself. This fear of abandonment caused me to abandon myself, my needs, and my principles.

There are consequences to abandoning yourself. Next thing that I knew was that I was homeless. I was living off of the streets and each time I gave my body to someone else for a cheap price, I was abandoning myself. I became more loyal to drugs than myself. I say cheap price because who can put a price on this holy temple? I was putting myself

The Woman with the Issue of Drugs

in some dangerous situations out of my loyalty to a toxic man and a toxic habit. Something began to stir in me to desire change. You are worth more than drugs. You are worth more than the toxicity. The Bible states, "What shall it profit a man, if he gains the entire world and loses his own soul? What can a man give in exchange for his soul?" Your soul is worth more than anything that this world has to offer. Don't abandon your soul for earthly pleasures. I did not realize how valuable that I was to God. Because I did not realize my value, I sunk deeper into the sin and perversion that I was in. I was hungry for change in my life.

I tried everything I knew to get off the crack cocaine. Rehab did not work because I did not have a support group after I got out of rehab. I was isolated from those that loved me and cared for me. I burnt so many bridges. I would miraculously get hired for jobs, but I would lose these jobs due to the bad environment that I was in. It was not cool to stay employed. In my crowd, destroying your life was acceptable. But doing something constructive with your life was looked down upon. To try to succeed meant more distance from the group. To fail was to be loved. Escaping the crab bucket is not easy. The moment you start climbing towards success, people reach up to drag you back down. There was a time that I got so high that I was repeatedly raped and assaulted. After the continued assaults it was common for me to sink into a deep depression. The only thing that would help me to move on was forgetting what happened. How did I forget what happened? Getting high on crack again. I was in a cycle and I was desperate for change. I was surprised at how quick my life turned downhill. There were several days that I did not sleep because I was constantly high. Subconsciously I was still carrying the death of my mom in my mind. I was truly grieving, but life was not slowing down. I was battling with shame because of how I abandoned my nephew. I never told my nephew that I was leaving, I just left. The sting of how I treated people that loved me truly began to weigh on my heart.

Things finally began to head in the right direction after meeting a man named Ricky. He was a womanizer, but he wouldn't use drugs. He had recently lost this wife and he was searching for constant companionship. I am not sure why he wanted women on drugs. I am sure he was trying to grieve in his own way just like I was. Ricky treated me very differently than other women. He was very kind to me. His awareness was very attractive to me because some-how he knew that I needed rest. He took me to his grandmother's home. He admonished me that I could not drink or smoke at her house because she was a Christian.

So, I did just that because I needed to rest. When I went to sleep, I had a dream of him taking me over to this lady's house. In the dream, I saw that when I walked into her house, there was a crystal ball in the middle of her kitchen table, and that I would live with her for three days. Often, whenever I dream of something, it literally happens just as I dreamed or close to it. When I woke up the next day, his grandmother had fixed breakfast for me, and he came to pick me up. When I got into the car, he mentioned that he wanted to take me over to this lady's house who was a Pastor. Her name was Mother Traywick, and he said that I should go stay with her for at least three days so she could help me. When I walked into her house, it was exactly like the dream I had the night before. But the difference was that the "crystal ball" on her table was a Bible—and instead of staying three days, I stayed for three months. She was the sweetest lady I ever met. She loved me back to myself. I got a job and then got my own place near her. I reunited with my family again and told them I was living in Hinesville, GA. She taught me a few things about the Bible, and she would have church in a small building at least twice a month. I did not learn anything about deliverance, but she taught me the love of Christ and how to love people.

Everything began to change in my life after discovering the love of God. I began to realize that his love was unconditional and that he loved me in spite of my issues. Although I do not believe that I was completely delivered. The love of God began to set me on a positive trajectory. I purchased a vehicle and I started working consistently. Once I was living by myself again, I began to drink alcohol again. Thankfully, I stayed away from drugs but this was a slippery slope. Mother Traywick would still come down to my trailer and check on me. But I was hiding my drinking from her. Then one day, after drinking about 6 cans of 8 Ball Malt liquor. Something spoke to me and said, "Just take a drive and chill out." That alcohol was talking to me, and I got in my car to go hang out with a few friends from work, but ended up getting stopped by the police and was arrested for DUI. Have you ever taken three steps forward and then five steps backward? No matter how much I tried to fix my life, it seemed that I was always getting into something. Mother Traywick came to bail me out of jail. That was the first of many arrests to follow. A few months after my arrest, Mother Traywick got sick. She went to move in with her brother in another town, and I lost contact with her. When I lost contact with Mother Traywick, I completely stopped going to church, and my downward spiral began all over again. Not only did the downward spiral begin, but also it triggered the emotions of loss within me again. It felt like I lost my mother again. Mother Traywick treated me as her daughter.

She was such a kind lady, and she taught me so much about the Bible that I did not know. I wish I had more time with her. She was an angel sent by God. Mother Traywick was even introduced to some of my family members, and they found her to be a precious jewel as well, not realizing that it had created a devastating blow for me to lose contact with her. I had stopped going to church. I began to drift towards my old life again. Something within me began to search for the same crowd of people that had issues with drugs. It is amazing that whatever our weakness is, that is what we are attracted to. It is so true, that birds of a feather flock together. I began to find the same crowd of people. I met this couple who were drug dealers, but they were friendly people. We became friend, and I visited them on the weekend. Which led me to smoking weed again. I needed to be delivered from the enemy within. Something in me was broken that only God could fix.

This couple reminded me of the times I used to have back when I was young, smoking weed, drinking, and sitting around eating and having a good time. The more I got close to them, I got addicted to crack. Then I found out they were drug dealers, but you wouldn't know it because they were the nicest people you ever met, and they were very low-key with how they sold drugs. Eventually, I found out they sold cocaine, but I was just trying to smoke weed and drink, and I did not want to get back on crack. I went over to their house one

The Woman with the Issue of Drugs

day to buy some weed. The lady went into the room to get me the weed and prepared the package to sell me the marijuana as I waited, she gave me the remote control to turn on the TV because she said it would be a while so I started flipping through her television, just watching random stuff. I ran across a documentary where they were showing people smoking crack cocaine. I immediately turned the channel, but a strong force caused me to turn back and watch it. I was mesmerized by watching the smoke fill the inside of the crack pipe, realizing that it was a high within itself, seeing the smoke. As I watched the lady smoke the cocaine through a crack pipe, I was hooked watching this documentary. The longer she took to come out of that room the more of a desire I started developing for crack cocaine again. By the time she came into the room to bring me the weed. I begged her to give me some cocaine. Because watching that documentary gave me a strong urge to start smoking again, and that very night, I opened the portal again and started back smoking crack cocaine. I now realize how important it is to guard your eye gates. I lost contact with Mother Traywick and wasn't going to church my house was open again to the enemy and I became worse off than I was the very first time I got addicted to drugs.

This made me realize that until you are free on the inside, you can move to a faraway country, but still find those same places and people. A lot of people dress the part on the outside, but are still dirty on the inside. It reminds me of the scripture where Jesus talks about the blind Pharisee, "How terrible it will be for you, legal experts and Pharisees! Hypocrites! You clean the outside of the cup and plate, but inside, they are full of violence and pleasure seeking. Blind Pharisee! First, clean the inside of the cup so that the outside of the cup will be clean too" (Matthew 23:22-26). Everywhere I ran, I always ended up finding the same people. I had not been delivered on the inside, even though I had gotten clean, started working again, and had my own place. Still, I had not been delivered and truly set free from the issue of drugs.

After trying everything, I realized that I was getting worse. I needed God more than anything. I could not lean on Mother Traywick's relationship with God, I needed an encounter for myself. Nothing else could satisfy, but the power of God and the blood of Jesus Christ. I felt unqualified and unclean, but I could hear his voice calling me. This woman had an issue of blood that cut her off from the community, I had an issue of drugs that cut me off from my community. All of the relationships that I valued were suffering because of my addiction. No relationship could heal me of my loneliness. No drug could satisfy the longing in my heart. No high could take away the emptiness within me. I needed a touch from God. I needed a move of God in my life. I needed a conversion experience.

3

FROM PERVERSION TO POWER

When the unclean spirit is gone out of a man, he walketh through dry places, seeking rest, and findeth none. Then he saith, I will return into my house from whence I came out; and when he is come, he findeth it empty, swept, and garnished. Then goeth he, and taketh with himself seven other spirits more wicked than himself, and they enter in and dwell there: and the last state of that man is worse than the first.

MATTHEW 12:44-45

I had a girlfriend, her name was Tina, and we stayed in the hotels together. We would get together just to have regular customers and clients. So, my girlfriend Tina and I used to have a regular client named Ted. He used to come over to my hotel room every weekend to get high. He would spend thousands of dollars because he worked for Gulfstream, and they made a lot of money. We also used to have clients who worked on the dock called Long Sherman, so there was plenty of money out there. Those men would come and get high with us and Ted was a regular. I was up for three nights without sleep. That's what cocaine does, it keeps you going. You don't want to eat or sleep.

Tina was the one who got with Ted, and they were just smoking crack. Supposedly Tina was to have sex with him, but Ted couldn't do anything because he was getting high, and so he couldn't perform. I must've fallen asleep because I woke up to a gun pressing against my temple, and I could feel the cold metal resting on my head, and I looked up, and it was Ted. He said you're going to get up and do what Tina didn't do and have sex with me. I had no fear out there in the streets, and I slapped the gun off my temple and told him Ted, "You better get that gun off me and I said we'll go find Tina. And so, we started walking to the door. And I opened the door to head down to the side of the hotel to see where Tina was. But she was coming towards the room with a guy named Neal, and suddenly, Ted started arguing with Neal and got very angry. He said, "I know she's not coming around with this guy." I had never seen Ted like that because he seemed mild mannered. I told Neal to go back to where he came from. From the look on their faces, they had beef with one another.

Neal was the one who would bully and rob people, so he must've robbed Ted, and he was mad about that. After Neal left, I said to Tina "You need to come inside and handle your business with Ted so he can go home. So, of course, when she went in with him, he couldn't perform at all, and he was still visibly upset, saying that Neal was the guy who robbed him, and he was going to get him, and Tina was like I've got to go. So, she left, and I just told Ted to calm down. I said, "Ted, you have a good job. You are here with us every weekend. We will be here. Come back next weekend. Go home. I told him to get some rest, and he agreed, saying, "Okay, Angela, you're right, you're right." So, he left.

But just a couple of hours later. The sun was setting; it was almost dark. All of a sudden, three guys came around the corner with guns pointed straight at me because I was sitting outside the hotel. They were like. "Where is she? I'm going to kill you if you don't tell me where they went." I was like, "Hold up, they went that way," but I pointed in the opposite direction because I didn't want them to shoot Tina. I ran inside my hotel room, and I closed the door, and I started putting chairs and the hotel table up against the door. I put up anything I could find to the door, anything that wasn't bolted down. Anything that was not nailed down became a part of my wall of protection. I just listened, and all of a sudden, I heard one gunshot. Then, it was like a couple of minutes that went by, and then all of a sudden, I heard pow, pow, pow, pow. I think it was four or five times.

Then I really got scared, and I just sat there, anticipating that they would come at me, but I waited. I ran into the back of the hotel because it was similar to a suite. I went into the back of the room, and I would listen to things, but I couldn't hear anything because it was like an eerie silence. Suddenly, everything was silent, and I must've fallen asleep. I don't know how soon it was. It could've been 20 minutes. It could've been an hour or several hours. I don't know because I had been up for days. But all I remember that morning is waking up to this loud bang at the door. It was the cop busting down the door with a gun drawn at me, yelling, "Get up, get up. We're going to take you down for murder." I was like, "Murder? I haven't done nothing," but when they got me downtown and got me inside the interrogation room, started questioning me saying, "You are to go down for murder if you don't tell us the truth." So, I told the truth, I said to them that Ted came with two other guys with guns, and they came looking for Neal because they had just got into an argument about Neal robbing Ted. I told Neal to leave, and I calmed Ted down and told him to go home and come back next weekend. Ted came back when the sun was setting, two other guys, including Ted, with guns pointing at me, asking me where Neal and Tina went. I said I told them in the opposite direction, and I ran into the room. I closed the door and barricaded myself inside the room. The cops said to me, "We know what you guys are doing out here with those drugs. We do not want the drugs, we want you to tell us the truth." Are you sure that it was Ted and two other guys?" I said, "I don't know the other guy's name, but I know that it was Ted. He worked at Gulfstream. I know that much, and they wrote out the information, and that's when I saw Nina in the other room. I realized she was alive because I didn't know who got shot that night, but the cops said that Neal got shot last night and died. The cops released us and told us we would have to testify at trial. If you are facing life, you will sing like a bird and that is what I did. I felt I was already dead because of how I was living.

When we got back to the room, Tina and I were still kind of shaken up about going out to the police department under the pretense of murder charges. But you know what, we went right back there trying to find some more dope and start getting high again.

These traumatic events pushed me deeper into drugs. Then we found out that Ted and the other boys were threatening to kill us because we snitched on Ted, yet we stayed out there getting high, moving from motel to motel. Still, I stayed because that drug kept me out there. Ted was eventually arrested, then he put a hit out for us, and his two friends were looking for us. But again, it was as if I had no fear. We stayed out there. One hit is a million too many, and a million hits are not enough.

When I got back on drugs, after my second arrest, I became worse off than before. I started hanging out with ruthless drug dealers and running the streets, robbing, and scheming with everybody I ran into. During those times, I ran into doctors, lawyers, and police officers, who requested weird fantasy encounters. There are some real-life freaks out there. During this time, I started a homosexual relationship with this girl. At first, it felt like I was being raped all over again. Initially, it did not feel right. It honestly felt unnatural to me. However, the drugs and running all night keep you numb to the things around you. Drugs truly numb your awareness. Eventually, the relationship started to feel good. The more I persisted and resisted my conscious, the better things began to feel. There was a tug of war within me. My mind knew something was wrong. My heart knew something was wrong. But my flesh was enjoying the relationship. Things began to get more confusing for me. The more I did things my way, the more confused I became. I started to enjoy the relationship with the woman more than I did being with a man due to the past abuse that I had encountered. This confusion began to feel like perversion. The enemy was trying to kill me; he came to kill, steal, and destroy. This relationship continued for a couple of years and I began to call good things evil and evil things good. Because it felt good. In this season of my life, I realized that I must be careful with feelings. Feelings can truly deceive. I continued down a terrible road of pain, heartache, sin, and rebellion.

I began to wonder where these feelings of confusion and rebellion originated. I remembered when I was 18 years old during basic training how one of my drill sergeants assaulted me. The more I began to think about this the more I realized that at every stage of my life men have assaulted me. Since I was 13 years old, being assaulted by men became expected. The devil began to make me view men in a horrid way. I was taken advantage of so much that the enemy made me believe that my refuge should be taken in relationships with women instead of men. I continued entertaining drugs to drown out the internal cries for help. Something within me was screaming for help, but I surrounded myself with noise. I drowned out the cries of trauma with more perversion. More sin. More rebellion. My actions constantly left me in a state of confusion. But how many know feelings will get you into trouble? The enemy does not have any new tricks, simply different faces and places. The child or person who is molested is quite confused when their body responds to the situation. This is how predators keep children, boys and girls, bound. They are confused because their body responds to it.

When you are dealing with the spirit of perversion, you have no idea of the lingering consequences it will have on you. I was so confused about why my body was responding to those acts. I also went through mental health issues because I had almost lost my mind out there in the world. Issues such as anxiety, depression, and low self-esteem. Feeling of shame, guilt, and self-hatred. I was not sure if I could ever recover from this. It had caused me to even experience problems with masturbation. Sexual perversion is running rapidly today, and it is even in church. People are afraid of getting help because they are ashamed. The devil loves for us to live in shame. The more we think upon and dwell upon shame, the more we are bound. We don't want to confess our sin because we are afraid of how others will perceive us. That is one of the problems with social media today. Everyone wants to present a perfect image and it delays our healing. It delays our transparency and honesty. This shame causes us to live with masks, but we cannot be delivered without truth and honesty.

I began to read my Bible and found this verse so captivating:

> Psalm 51:10, "Create in me, O God, a clean heart and renew a right spirit in me."

I would repeat that verse every day, and I noticed things changing in me. The gossip around the jail tables began to hurt my ears. I started going to bible study in jail. I wanted to understand how and why I lost my way. When I began to quote Psalm 51:10 every day, God would show me visions in my dreams of things that didn't please Him. I started to dislike everything about the way I was living. I had a girlfriend in prison, and one day we had a Bible study. I asked the teacher why God gives you these feelings of love towards the same sex and it feels right. Unaware of the internal change within me. I began to see and hear differently. The prison would let churches come in and teach bible study, and I remember asking in a Bible study class why sin feels good despite being wrong. Because I was dealing with those perverted spirit and I had my girlfriend with me. What I kept feeding, kept me bound.

The teacher responded and said God does not do that, he gives you a way of escape in 1 Corinthians 10:13. "God does not give you those feelings Satan does and your flesh. God provides a way of escape from temptation." God is faithful. He will give you a way of escape, so that ye may be able to bear it." How many know that feelings get you in trouble?

Some of y'all might remember that song "If loving you is wrong; I don't want to be right!" Songs like these are born from feelings that are not right. So, I started embracing God's word, and changes began occurring within me during my incarceration. The noise around me became unbearable. Though I didn't understand what God was doing. I simply knew I was changing. One day those lustful feelings arose in me, and I cried out to God, saying, "You said, and that teacher said, you will give me a way of escape, where my escape is?!" Suddenly, a gospel song came on. I cried out and found myself upstairs in my cell vomiting up this nasty green stuff that I knew had to be demonic in nature. I just felt something leave my body. I stayed in my cell, the remainder of the night, praying and reading my Bible. Unaware that God was delivering me, something demonic left me. I know I could feel it leave. Glory be to God!

God removed the scales from my eyes after a season of deep spiritual darkness. The very next day, I walked out of my cell and saw my so-called girlfriend—and what I saw was not the same. She looked like a demon. In that moment, I didn't second-guess it. I told her straight up: "Stay away from me—I am done." One thing I know now is that you cannot keep playing with something that God has revealed to you. Because when God opens your eyes, you don't argue with demons. You are supposed to rebuke and resist them. That moment in my life was the turning point for me. That is when I knew God was serious about pulling me out of my situation. And that's when my testimony began—not just that I heard God, but that I obeyed Him.

One thing I realized is that once I believed in God's word, it started to come alive to me. Feelings will get you in trouble. If anybody touches you the right way, your body will respond. It's a perverse love. People often say, "But we can love who we choose," and that is true. But what type of love is it? I had faith in what was written in the Bible. So, after learning the scriptures, I began to meditate on them. And lo and behold, I was tempted after I received the word from 1 Corinthians 10:13 about no temptation that overtakes us but such as is common to man. And I remember I was tempted, and those feelings started rising inside of me, and I cried out to God. If your word is true, why are these feelings rising inside of me? Lord, you said in your word there is no temptation taken but such as common to man, but you are faithful, you will not suffer us to be tempted above what we can handle. I gave God back his word because he is bound by his word, and it will never return to the void.

There was also another temptation that came to me. Now, the night before, I was reading my Bible. I was reading Genesis 39:11-12 (NIV): "One day he went into the house to attend to his duties, and none of the household servants was inside. She caught him by his cloak and said, 'Come to bed with me! But he left his cloak in her hand and ran out of the house. So, the next morning when I woke up, I heard God say, "Reread the story of Joseph." Not knowing the temptation that lay ahead of me, I thought to myself, "I just read this last night." Nevertheless, I reread it. After my morning devotion, I went downstairs to sit in the common area, carrying my Bible. Then another girl came up to me, who I knew liked me, but I was changing. She began to speak flattering words to me, and my flesh began to rise up in me because everyone wants to be loved, and I had not been totally delivered. So here I am showing her in my Bible, Romans Chapter 1, verses 25-32. All the while I'm trying to share this with her, she continues to flatter me with her words. Suddenly, I heard God say, "Run like Joseph ran." So, I did just that, and I left her and my Bible right on that table. There was another lady that I would study the Bible with all of the time. I would grab her Bible and bring it to my cell. That lady and the Bible helped me to flee from that girl. By the grace of God we kept that girl away from me. Late that night, at about 3 am, the guards knocked on my cell door to pack it up. They were shipping me out to the halfway. His word is true; he will make a way of escape for you. I knew then that I needed more deliverance, and it came. Flattering words can't move me anymore because I know the truth. And the Lord knew I could only run so far in jail, so he created a way of escape because I wasn't supposed to be shipped out until my second court date. Even the guards said that they had never transported someone at 3:00 AM. Especially before all of my court dates were even completed. But God!

Despite my sinful lifestyle, my faith in God remained. Then, on December 29, 2004, a police force raided the house we stayed in, and it resulted in yet another arrest for me. I was angry with God, a hypocritical reaction given my lifestyle of prostitution, homosexuality, promiscuous lifestyle and drug abuse. "But that arrest… that was the turning point in my life. Something was different this time. It wasn't like the other two times I'd been locked up—this time, I picked up the Word for myself. I started to really seek God, not just say His name. I began to believe in Him for real, and that's when everything started to change." How many know He is never far from us? God states in his word:

> Am I a God at hand, saith the Lord, and not a God afar off? Can any hide himself in secret places that I shall not see him? Saith the Lord. Do not I fill heaven and earth? Saith the Lord. Amen!!

I began to feel the power of God work in and through me. The demonic oppression left me and now it was time to pour the right things within me. It was not enough for me to be delivered and set free, my house was clean. I needed to pour the right things into my life. I began to pour the word of God and prayer into my life. I left no room for the enemy to come back in and capture me. The Bible states, "Let the thief who stole, steal no more but let him labor with his hands and give to the poor." It is not enough to stop stealing. The thief must replace the habit of stealing with labor. The thief must replace the habit of stealing with giving to the poor. If the thief stops stealing, but does not labor or give then the enemy still has an open door to come in. I began to experience the life transforming power of God.

When I sincerely repented to God that is when everything started changing for me. I did not want to live in sin. I was tired of this prison cell. Life finally broke me down. The prison finally made me cry for freedom. Psalm 51 was written by the greatest king in Israel. David made a huge mistake with Bathsheba by sleeping with her. Whenever he was rebuked for his sin, he repented. Repentance is the beginning of transformation. We can no longer pretend that everything is going good in our lives. We have to confess our sin and our disobedience to God. When I repented it prepared me to be baptized later. Whenever I was baptized it prepared the way for me to receive the Spirit of God. Faith and repentance laid for the foundation for God to do a miraculous work in my life. The perversion was gone. I began walking in the power of God.

4

THE GRAVEYARD

Therefore we are buried with him by baptism into death: that like as Christ was raised up from the dead by the glory of the Father, even so we also should walk in newness of life.

ROMANS 6:4 KJV

I want to show you how far God will go to get a hold of you. My life led me to going into graveyards. Before my ministry was birthed, I was in some nasty habits. I started lying and writing checks again to support my habit, and it got me into more trouble. I got arrested for the second time for forging checks. I was in jail, still hanging around the wrong people and listening to a lot of things that criminals talk about. In my mind, I wanted to get back to work and start afresh. Upon my second release from jail, I stayed in contact with a guy I knew back in Hinesville. I stayed in touch with this guy I knew back in Hinesville. He treated me right in the past, and he told me he would take care of me. He moved me across state lines in exchange for my help. Little did I realize he was trafficking me into being a housekeeper and to cook and clean for him and have sex with him, and he ended up trafficking me from Florida to Augusta, Ga. Since I was still homeless, he took advantage of that by making promises he did not keep. He lured me into getting with other men to bring them into the house so he could get them to spend all their money on drugs because they were users too. I had to keep the house clean, cook, wash clothes, and do everything he needed me to do, including entertaining folks he brought over, men and women. I kept thinking I had shelter and was no longer sleeping on the streets. I thought at least I had a bed to sleep in and food to eat. Little did I know he wanted more than I was willing to offer. So, one day, I told him I was going to make some money to buy more drugs from him. He was always okay with that because the more drugs he supplied to me; he knew I would return. But this time I did not come back, I just walked the streets, and it was so bad out there that I almost returned to him. I was able to escape from his hold on me. I was homeless, sleeping on park benches, recalling morning waking up with dew on me from sleeping outside, and sleeping on the floors of a drug crack house.

I ran into this guy that I knew from the streets, and I saw him around, and he said, "Do you want to get high?" I said, "Yeah." I was already drinking and so we started walking. It was dark, and I was high and drunk, so I wasn't paying attention. But it was like a driveway. I started seeing headstones and realized I was inside a graveyard. I said, "This is a graveyard." He said, "I know, but it's a shortcut to the dealer's house." Whenever we got deeper into the graveyard, he threw me down. I tried to run and fight him off, but as I got up to escape, all I could see were headstones surrounding me. I did not know which way to go. He caught me again and started beating me. At that moment, I stopped resisting—just trying to survive and find a way out. In the middle of that graveyard, he raped me. I just laid there next to graves being violently raped all over again. After I was assaulted, I could barely see anything. I was stumbling in the darkness and I could not find my way out. The whole scene was terrifying. Yet, I had to follow him out and he moved with ease through that graveyard, and that is when I realized this was not his first time. He knew exactly how to go in and how to get out. Yet I did not try to get help or get off drugs. That added another layer of trauma to my life. I wanted to kill myself out there by smoking and drinking because I did not have the nerve to just shoot myself, even though I felt like it many times.

One day, I was at this other drug house that was owned by a lady, and we would just call her Pat. So Pat was a drug dealer who also used drugs. But she would make so much money by letting people come over and use her place for drug use. "Come hang out with me," she said one afternoon, casual like always.

I didn't think much of it then. But later, I realized she didn't just want to hang out—she wanted me to stay. To be hers. The crazy part? I had just broken free from a man who dealt drugs and controlled everything I did. And now, somehow, I'd found myself tangled up with another drug dealer. Only this time, it was a woman—a friend, or so I thought. A friend with benefits… an unnatural friendship that blurred every line. How many know the devil has no new tricks, simply different faces, and places, that is all.

Free from the fear, the control, the chaos that came with being tied to a man who lived and breathed the drug game. But freedom can be tricky—it doesn't always lead you where you expect. So here I am, running from a male drug dealer, only to land straight into the hands of a woman drug dealer who wanted to use me the same way. Talking about leaving one dire situation and running right into a worse one. It felt like life was playing some cruel joke on me, showing me that danger doesn't always wear the same face. Amidst that relationship, she offered me all the crack I wanted—if I stayed with her. Even during all those perverse activities, I was still praying and unaware of God's constant presence. Ironically, I suggested to her that we are going to start watching church before getting high, a form of preaching, even as I planned to sin. But glory be to God, He was at work, saving me through the "foolishness of preaching." I had always prayed that the Lord would deliver me while I was out there.

God had to take me to another graveyard. I was baptized in Jesus' name. I was buried with Jesus Christ. I buried the old me and rose up as a new creature. God redeemed me. He redeemed the time.

Buried with him in baptism. Wherein also ye are risen with him through faith of the operation of God, who hath raised him from the dead. And you being dead in your sins and the uncircumcision of your flesh, hath he quickened together with him, having forgiven you all trespasses. Blotting out the handwriting of ordinances that was against us, which was contrary to us, and took it out of the way, nailing it to his cross (Colossians 2:12-14 KJV).

The enemy tried to use a graveyard to rape and traumatize me. But God brought me to a spiritual graveyard and buried the trauma and my sin. I identified with Jesus Christ burial. He was buried for me. He went to the graveyard for me. When I came up out of the waters of baptism, I felt a difference. I finally got a new beginning. I finally received a fresh start. God washed me and cleansed me. I do not have a single disease. Not one deadly disease infected me. God protected me and he put his name upon my soul. I am so thankful that Jesus went to the grave for me. He went to the grave to set me free. My past is over, I am new in the name of Jesus. It is never too late to give your life to God. You can become a new creature. When I came out of the waters of baptism, I felt that I had a purpose!

5

FROM GUILT TO GRACE

There is therefore now no condemnation to them which are in Christ Jesus, who walk not after the flesh, but after the Spirit.

ROMANS 8:1 KJV

The state of Georgia has me listed as a felon, but God has wiped the record clean, so I'm not guilty in his eyes, his blood has covered all my sins. So, I will always be free, no longer bound. Many miracles occurred during my incarceration. Women would come to me for prayer, and I would pray for them, and God would do a miracle in their cases. I had favor with all the guards and staff in the jail. I was able to win people to Christ while in jail.

God's favor was truly upon my life. He would place women in my path who had prophetic dreams about me—visions of what was to come and how God was shaping my future. It was as if He used their dreams to confirm what He had already whispered to my spirit, reminding me that his hand was on me even when I couldn't see the full picture. I remember the day I had to stand before the judge for a burglary charge—a serious crime that carried a sentence of 10 to 15 years. My heart was pounding because I knew the odds were not in my favor. To make matters worse, I found out that the very judge I was standing before had recently had his own home broken into. Talk about bad timing. To top it off, my public defender seemed completely uninterested in my case, as if my future didn't matter. I felt alone, helpless, and scared—like the whole world was stacked against me.

So, we finally went to court. I was sitting there, heart pounding, listening as the judge handed down sentence after sentence—ten years, fifteen years—all for people facing the same kind of charges I had. Then there was this one young man who caught my attention. He came before the judge dressed in his Navy uniform. He had gotten caught up with some friends while home on leave—breaking into houses in his neighborhood. His lawyer pleaded his case, explaining that he had already paid back the money and returned everything that was taken. But even with all that, the judge still sentenced him to ten years.

I sat there thinking, *Oh my God… if he received years, what's going to happen to me?* My heart sank, but deep down, I had already made up my mind—no matter what the outcome would be, I was going to serve the Lord. Whether it meant freedom or time behind bars, I was determined to trust God through it all.

However, the day before I was supposed to stand before that judge, something remarkable happened. While I was incarcerated, I met a lady there. She came up to me and said, "I had a dream about you. In the dream, you won your court case, and you didn't have to come back here to serve time in this jail in Hinesville, Georgia. You stayed in the Macon Diversion Center instead." The lady told me that in her dream, I had long hair, and that my lawyer would be removed from my case because God was going to give me favor. I believed every word she said, but I'll admit—I was a little confused about the part where she said I had long hair. At that time, my hair was short, so I couldn't quite see how that part would come to pass.

The courtroom was so packed that the judge didn't even get to my case—or another young lady's case. We were told to come back the next day. That next morning, they placed me in a holding cell with the same young lady who was also waiting to see that same judge. She went before me, and while I was sitting there waiting my turn, something unexpected happened—my lawyer, the one who hadn't been doing much for me anyway, got an emergency phone call and had to step out. Right then, they replaced him with a new lawyer. That's when it hit me—the dream was coming to life, just like she said. God was already setting things in order before I even stood before the judge.

The replacement lawyer they gave me was so kind—nothing like the one before. He actually took the time to sit down with me and talk about my case. After the young lady before me went into the judge's chambers and came back out, it was finally my turn to stand before the judge. My new lawyer began pleading my case, telling the judge how well I had been doing at the Macon Diversion Center—that I was working, staying out of trouble, and really trying to turn my life around.

Then the judge looked at me and asked, "Ms. Brown what happened? Why did you break into that house?" I told him the truth. I said, "Your Honor, it was a friend's house. They were out of town, and I had just been kicked out of my boyfriend's house. It was cold that January night, and I just needed a place to stay. I took a small TV to support my habit—I even cleaned their house and left my wallet and a note explaining what happened."

The judge looked at me hard, like he wasn't sure whether to believe me. I started crying, but I kept talking. Then suddenly, the District

Attorney threw his hands up and said, "Finally, someone comes in here and tells the truth!" He leaned over and whispered something to the judge and my lawyer. Then the judge looked back at me and said, "Ms. Brown I'm going to allow you to continue serving your time at the Diversion Center instead of sentencing you to ten years in prison. The DA has agreed to drop the burglary charge and reduce it to theft by taking—because you told the truth. I broke down in tears right there in that courtroom. I had watched this same judge give out ten- and fifteen-year sentences all day long for the same charge—but God's favor rested on me that day.

So, after court, I headed back to the holding cell with the young lady who had gone before me. We were waiting for transportation to take us back to jail. As we sat there, the judge, the DA, and my new lawyer walked by our cell. The judge stopped, looked right at me, and said, "Ms. Brown talk to that young lady about telling the truth." I just nodded and said, "Yes Sir." Once they walked out of sight, I turned to the young lady and asked what had happened. She looked at me and said, "I lied to them—and they had me on a recorded phone line." That moment hit me hard. It truly *pays to tell the truth*. A few minutes later, one of the court clerks—the same one sitting in the judge chamber and records everything—walked past our cell. She stopped, looked at me, and said, "Ms. Brown I'm a Christian, and I want you to know something. In all my years serving in this courtroom, I've never witnessed anything like what I saw when you walked in. The glory of the Lord came in with you. I could feel it and see it. God is with you." When I got back to my jail cell, I shared all of this with the lady who had dreamed about me earlier. I told her how her dream had come to pass, just like she said it would. Then I asked her about the part of the dream where she said I had long hair, because at that time, my hair was short. That's when it came back to both of our remembrance—the Scripture that says:

> "But if a woman have long hair, it is a glory to her: for her hair is given her for a covering." (1 Corinthians 11:15, KJV).

At that moment, I just began to weep. The court clerk said she saw *the glory* of the Lord with me—and that Scripture reminded me that His glory truly was my covering. Glory be to God! He brought me out of darkness into His marvelous light—from a foolish woman to a wise woman. Amen.

Whenever people find out I'm from Florida, they often ask, "Why did you move to Georgia?" And my answer is always the same: *The Lord sentenced me here.* You see, the judge had me sent to the Macon Diversion Center, a women's halfway house in Macon, GA. At the time, I was locked up in Augusta, GA, which also had a halfway house—but God knew exactly where I needed to be.

While at the Macon Diversion Center, I began praying for a church that preached the truth. God led me to one. Even while I was still at the halfway house, He baptized me with the Holy Ghost evidenced by speaking in other tongues. Filled with God's power, I knew I could resist the devil, and my soul caught fire for Him. From that moment on, I began sharing my testimony and winning souls for Christ.

I remember one day I invited thirteen women from the Diversion Center to come to church with me. The warden couldn't believe it and started interrogating me, thinking we were just trying to find a way out of the center. But I knew the truth—God was moving in my life to be a soul winner for Jesus. I don't boast about my past iniquities or the perverted lifestyle I once lived, but I do testify about the God who delivers from darkness. Even with a record of five felonies—cocaine possession, theft, and three forgery charges—God's light found me. His grace reached me in the darkest moments, and He blessed me beyond measure God blessed me with a federal job at Robins Air Force Base, complete with a secret clearance, and I've been there for fourteen years now. Through His favor, I was even able to buy back six years of active duty, and this year, I celebrated a total of twenty years of service—fourteen years in the Air Force and six years in the Army. Over these years, I've received seven promotions. My cup truly is running over… Who can do that but God?

6

THE MIRACLE OF MINISTRY

And they overcame him by the blood of the Lamb, and by the word of their testimony; and they loved not their lives unto death.

REVELATION 12:11 KJV

God was opening so many doors for me, it was amazing to witness. While God was cleansing and delivering me, he began to use me for his glory. I felt so unworthy of being used by God. One of the main reasons for feeling unworthy was my battle with temptation. Even with the power of God within me, temptation is a never-ending war. Thankfully, temptation is not a sin. Jesus Christ was tempted at all points as we were, but he remained without sin. When a temptation comes it is important to immediately give it to Jesus. Satan wants us to walk defeated as if we have already sinned whenever the thought crosses our minds. But that is a lie. I am not my thoughts. You are not your thoughts. We are not our thoughts. Our identity is in Christ, not in anything else. I struggled with nonstop temptation after I decided that I was done with the world.

Even filled with the Holy Ghost, temptation is a never-ending war. We are all tempted in one way or another, but it is up to us to yield or resist it.

"I find then a law, that, when I do good, evil is present with me. For I delight in the law of God after the inward man: But I see another law in my members, warring against the law of my mind, and bringing me into captivity to the law of sin which is in my members.

O wretched man that I am! Who shall deliver me from the body of this death? I thank God through Jesus Christ our Lord. So then, with the mind I serve the law of God, but with the flesh the law of sin" (Romans 7:21-25).

I was still struggling with masturbating because I thought to myself, since I wasn't having sex with anyone else, how could I possibly be sinning? It wasn't until God opened my eyes to the teaching I was receiving at my church. Because to be honest, most churches don't talk about this issue; they just tell you to pray about it. How to deal with it while you are waiting for your prayer to be answered. More churches really need to talk about this issue because so many people are dying on the pews because they can't fully express themselves and their struggles. I am so grateful for my church, Apostolic of Byron, Ga (AOB). It's a safe place and we learn about all these sexual struggles that most folks encounter. We are taught that there is a way of escape.

> "There hath no temptation taken you but such as is common to man: but God is faithful, who will not suffer you to be tempted above that ye are" (1 Corinthians 10:13).

We have this raw conversation in our roundtable talks at our church. Many have been set free by this teaching. After receiving the teaching, I was able to wrestle with that demon, and I won. Let me explain, every Sunday I would go to the altar after sinning and lift my hands praising the Lord, even if I committed masturbation that week or the night before. I would hear the enemy whisper in my ear, "I know what you did last night." Because he is the accuser of the brother. Revelation 12:10: This verse describes the devil (often referred to as

Satan) as "the accuser of our brothers and sisters, who accuses them before our God Day and night." I was so determined after learning how to fight. I would tell them enemy, I don't care, because when I'm free, you will see what I will do with you after my deliverance.... crushing your head with my feet. So, one day I wrestled with that perverted demon all day and night. I must have finally fallen asleep. Still, when I woke, I saw a greyish-looking silhouette walk in front of my bed, and I heard the Lord say, "Get up and open your door, and command that spirit to leave." I did just that. It was late, around 2 AM, and I recall walking back into my bedroom and turning on the light. My room looked like a tornado had come through it. I was fighting that demon after it came to attack me in my sleep. Some of you today have those weird sexual dreams, it is so important to check our spirit. God can free us from anything. There is a song that goes like this: "Me and the devil had a tussle, but I won. I hate him and I know he hates me. Me and him, we don't agree. Me and the devil had a tussle, but I won. That's exactly what happened that night. I won! Glory be to God! Do not allow the enemy to tear you down with worry and condemnation. There is no condemnation in Jesus Christ. Through his blood, we win. The Bible states, "We overcome by the blood of the lamb and by the word of our testimony." He delivered us through the blood and my testimony is one of millions that is equipping you to be set free by the power of God. When God delivers you from the mess, he is birthing a ministry within you. It is miraculous that God would want to bring a ministry out of me.

After I share my testimony and speak at events, audience members and church attendees frequently ask me in private how I can discuss so much personal information publicly. I give the same answer,

"Because I am free!" That is what I was then, and this is me now, and all my sins are under the blood. God has given me the boldness to say I am no longer bound. Who the son sets free is free indeed.

I am writing this book because the Lord told me that many will be set free through my story. However, it took me a while because others mocked me and spread negative comments about me sharing personal details from my past. Even some church folks gossip about me, so why should I share such graphic details of my past? I realized that they are just feeling uncomfortable about their own struggles and experience. You have young men and women now in church battling with perversion, pornography, promiscuity, and whatever else the world is offering. Dying on the pew because they cannot share their struggles in a safe place because they see us church folks all polished and clean. People wrongly believe that they cannot be free because no one in the church talks about these things.

This is why I'm so grateful to have a church, Apostolics of Byron located in Byron, Ga. We take our time to talk about these sexual desires and unnatural sex in a safe place through a biblical and godly lens. So, I will continue to share my testimony because of the boldness God has given me to help others overcome guilt and shame. The blood is more than enough, but through our testimony we are burying the devil where he belongs.

I remember going into prayer crying to God about sharing my stories, and I told him I do not want to share them anymore. And God said to me, "They are not mocking you, my daughter, because I died for you, and they are mocking me, and woe be unto them." Vengeance is the Lord's. Some people may mock or gossip about me. But he has covered my sins with his blood. There is nothing sweet about sin, so why should I try to sugarcoat my testimony? Sin is ugly, and it separates you from God.

Isaiah 64:6 (NIV) "All of us have become like one who is unclean, and all our righteous acts are like filthy rags."

This shows that sin contaminates everything, even our best efforts apart from God. Sin also deceives and enslaves us John 8:34: "Jesus replied, 'Very truly I tell you, everyone who sins is a slave to sin."

Sin traps people, promising pleasure but leading to bondage. I do not glory in my past sin, but I glory in God's redeeming power. I am simply redeemed.

God had a plan for my life before the foundation of this earth.

Ephesians 1:4 states, "According as he hath chosen us in him before the foundation of the world, that we should be holy and without blame before him in love."

Jeremiah 1:5 tells us, "Before I formed you in the womb, I knew you, and before you were born, I consecrated you."

What I went through in my past was never who I was supposed to be. I am living the life that he created for me right now. I blame no one for my experience and the choices I made because I put myself in those situations. I chose to ignore all the warning signs before my self-destruction. I recall my time in prison. I had just turned 40 years old, and I took a serious look at my life. I had lost everything. What was I doing here? I started to wise up, and I cried out to God, setting in motion a profound spiritual awakening. I started reading the Bible, and I memorized Psalm 51:10: "Create in me a clean heart, O God, and renew a right spirit within me." No matter how God uses me in ministry, I keep this prayer of repentance close to my heart. I do not take where I am in life for granted. God gave me a second chance at life and I do not plan to waste it.

I serve as the singles director at our church, and one of the things I'm most proud of is our "Round Table Talks." These gatherings are unlike anything I've ever experienced in a church setting. We come together—men and women, single and searching, waiting and wondering—and we talk. Really talk. There's no judgment, no pretending. We discuss the things most people are too afraid to say out loud in church—our sexual desires, our struggles, the tug-of-war between spirit and flesh. It's raw and unfiltered, but it's also sacred. Because it's a safe place. I will never forget one meeting. We had a visitor come to our event, and this was her testimony: she thought she was the only one sitting silently on the pew, dealing with these feelings. Condemnations had taken over her mind because she was afraid of speaking out about it. There is such liberty in confession your fault one to another. Bishop Williams sits with us, steady and wise, guiding every conversation back to the Word of God. He reminds us that God created marriage between a man and a woman—not to be ashamed of our feelings, but to show us where they belong, how they can be honored. He tells us, "You are okay to have those feelings. God made you human." He reminds us that perversion sets in whenever sex is outside the covenant of marriage. Committing adultery and fornication with man or woman is not of God. It is not God's design for us.

Sin is sin, and they all separate you from God. It took me years, I am talking years, to be free from all those dreams and the stench of perversion because of all the assaults I had encountered and the portal I opened up while out there on drugs.

This is why I can write this book. People may mock me or look at me differently, but glory be to God, I am free. I am no longer bound. For me personally, I have come to understand my own sexuality and its relationship to my faith in a special way. We live in a world today where people do not know the difference or cannot identify who a woman is. I once believed that my physical attraction to the same sex meant it was love. But through my faith journey, I've come to see it as something different – something I now understand as "perverse love." That's just my experience and interpretation. The most important thing I want to emphasize is that I love everyone, including those who identify as homosexual and any other sexual sin. Her, Him, She, He, them, cat, or dog. That is your belief, and you are free to do as you please. Because God has given us free will and choice. It's up to us to choose ye this day whom we will serve, and as for me and my household, we will serve the Lord. I love people, but I do not have to love sin and their version of truth. I simply don't condone the act, based on my personal beliefs, faith, and experience. I chose God's words over my feelings.

When I share my story, people often ask me if I really did all this stuff, then why am I sharing now? The enemy did not want me to write this book. Because the enemy put thoughts in my mind that people would judge me. I kept hearing God say, "Continue to write and share, because many people will be blessed by your story." There are a lot of saved people sitting in church dealing with these same issues concerning perversion and pornography. There are people who have a spouse dealing with the same problems, but are afraid to confess and get help. I have traveled throughout the state of Georgia sharing my testimony. Every time I finish sharing my testimony, someone always pulls me to the side and whispers that they are either dealing with it or they have a child dealing with it. That's the miracle of ministry, I am still alive to share my story. I am alive to speak boldly about my freedom. I'm no longer bound. I have been set free by the word of my testimony and by the blood of the lamb. The truth shall make you free.

The Lord has given me grace and wisdom to win souls just by telling my testimony. This is why it's important to share your testimony with others so they can see that God is real. God has also allowed me to work with different organizations that help women, children, and even men escape the life of being trafficked for sex or being abused by men and women who exploit them.

I appreciate the system for allowing faith-based programs to continue, such as the one my mentors taught at the Macon Day reporting in their character development class. Most jobs today require you to have completed intervention programs and classes, especially if you have a criminal background. This is typically achieved by completing all the courses at the Macon Diversion Center and the Macon Day reporting center. It allowed me to get a good-paying job. We need more faith-based programs because when the heart is changed, the mind is changed. Once I allowed Jesus to get a hold of me. I did not want to live the way I was living anymore. The Bible tells us that:

> Therefore, if any man be in Christ, he is a new creature: old things are passed away (2 Corinthians 5:17).

My mentors also taught a course called Spirit of Freedom of Ministries. It is a Christian intervention program that offers a lot to a person. I was privileged to be a part of that program. Upon completion of the course, I became a teacher. I have witnessed lives come through that program from the federal prison system, totally transformed. When I was released from the Diversion Center in 2007. I remained faithful to my church and followed all the rules that are required of me as a probationer. I was blessed to get a job at Perdue Farms, and from there, I'm now employed at Robins Air Force Base. I have received several promotions since I was hired by the Defense Logistics Agency, Defense Logistics Aviation, and now I'm with the Air Force at Robins Air Base with a secret security clearance. There are many good programs out there that can help a person in recovery. But the one thing I know for sure is you must keep Jesus in the forefront.

I have worked with judges, probation officers, and police officers in the local community. God has opened doors for me to share my testimony at places beyond what I could have imagined. The guest speaker at the "GPSTC" Georgia Public Safety Training Center for probation officers in Forsyth, GA, gave me the chance to speak at Pulaski State Prison and Central State Prison. I have been able to share my story all over the state of Georgia. The miracle of ministry is that the wretched woman I was, God was able to turn me around and use me for his glory. I have been ordained as an Evangelist, and the Lord has allowed me to become the Singles Director at my local church. John Chapter 4:29: "Come see a man. This is why I say,' Come to Jesus. 'Come see a man who has told me all about myself. "This lady won a whole city to the Lord because he exposed her nakedness. She ran and told the entire town, and they all came out because she was exposed by Jesus' word. This is why I tell my story. I want to win souls to the Lord, and I want people to know that he is no respecter of people. If he can do it for me, he can do it for you. Jesus met me the well, and I was made whole, and to this day, I'm running and telling my story to win an entire city, town, and region.

The woman at the well was rejected and living in a life of sin cut off from the community. But after and encounter with Christ, she was able to testify about the goodness of God. In one moment, she became an evangelist for the Lord. Her testimony prepared the way for Philip in the book of Acts. When he preached many were baptized in the name of the Lord and later many received the Spirit of God. It all started with one lady that was willing to share her testimony.

I will never get tired of telling my testimony, and you shouldn't either. We all have a testimony, and it is the Word of our Testimony and the Blood of the Lamb that we are overcome. He is King and Lord of all, deserving all honor and glory. He kept me from deadly diseases and death. That alone is the Grace of God. As we read the list of Jesus' ancestors, it is encouraging to see that they include Tamar (the adulteress), Rahab (the prostitute), Ruth (the non-Jewish Moabite),

Solomon (who was conceived after King David's adulterous affair with Bathsheba), as well as many others.

Thankfully, God uses sinful human beings and, therefore, can use us. Whatever your past, however broken your life may seem right now, God can use you to do something great with your life. The very name 'Jesus' means, 'he will save his people from their sins' (v.21). Every time we use the name Jesus, it reminds us that our greatest need is not for happiness or contentment (although these may both be by-products). Our greatest need, as with Jesus' ancestors, is for forgiveness. Therefore, we need a Savior.

As you read my story, God has always been with me every step of the way. The shame will keep you out there, but God's love will draw you to repent. John 15:16 NIV states: "You did not choose me, but I chose you and appointed you so that you might go and bear fruit—fruit that will last—and so that whatever you ask in my name the father will give you." When I first read this scripture, I was still in prison. An elderly lady came in to teach Bible study, and she talked from this scripture. When she read it to us, I just started weeping because here I was a prostitute, adulteress, a drug addict, a thief, and a liar, and God chose me? I must have cried all night, tears of appreciation for how deep God's love is towards us. He called me out of darkness into his marvelous light. I am simply redeemed.

You have a story to tell the world. Do not be ashamed of your testimony. You did not go through it for nothing. You did not fight these battles for no reason. God is going to bring your story and your message to the world. Let my story give you hope. Allow my story to inspire you. God can get glory out of your life. No matter how hard the prison has been. No matter how hard the journey has been. God will cultivate purpose out of it. God is going to bury your past exactly like he buried mine. God is your redeemer. You are redeemed. We are simply redeemed.

ABOUT THE AUTHOR

Evangelist Angela Brown's journey of salvation began in 2005 while she was incarcerated. In her search for truth, God filled her with the precious gift of the Holy Ghost, and her life was forever changed for the glory of God. Old things passed away, and she became a new creature in Christ Jesus. She is a faithful member of Apostolics of Byron, Georgia, under the leadership of Bishop Dominic Williams. Appointed as the Singles Director, she leads a thriving Singles Ministry and passionately teaches and lives according to God's ordinances concerning singleness.

A proud veteran, Evangelist Brown has the unique distinction of serving in the U.S. Army and working as a civilian in the U.S. Air Force. Beyond her military service, she is deeply committed to outreach and serves with formally known as Out of Darkness and now is The Freedom Collective an anti-trafficking ministry dedicated to rescuing and restoring women and children affected by the sex-trafficking industry. Her calling has opened doors to share her testimony across Georgia at churches, prisons, schools, and community events. She has spoken at Pulaski State Prison, Central State Prison, and Southwest High School in Macon, Georgia. She has also been a featured guest on Restoring Broken Vessels on WGNM Christian Television and interviewed on WGXA News Channel 24 in Macon, Georgia. Evangelist Brown was invited as a guest speaker at the Georgia Public Safety Training Center (GPSTC) in Forsyth, Georgia, where she addressed probation officers about the power of restoration and hope. Her ministry is fueled by the conviction that God still has the power to save, heal, and deliver. She believes no situation is beyond His reach, and she boldly declares the gospel wherever God sends her. Her favorite scripture is Psalm 51:10: "Create in me a clean heart, O God; and renew a right spirit within me." Evangelist Angela Brown's greatest passion is traveling and sharing the good news of Jesus Christ. With a special heartbeat and anointing for winning souls, she continues to proclaim the message of God's love, grace, and saving power to a world in need of hope.

www.ingramcontent.com/pod-product-compliance
Lightning Source LLC
Chambersburg PA
CBHW070631050426
42450CB00011B/3160